Shining Stars
A Collection of Poetry by the pupils of
Clyro School

With foreword by Gwyneth Lewis,
National Poet of Wales

CONTENTS BY THE CHILDREN OF
CLYRO SCHOOL

All rights reserved

© The contributors, 2005

The right of the contributors to be identified as the authors of this work has been asserted by them in accordance with Section 77 of the Copyright, Designs and Patents Act 1988.

This book is copyright. Subject to statutory exception and to provisions of relevant collective licensing agreements, no reproduction of any part may take place without the written permission of Clyro School

First published 2005

Published by TheSchoolBook.com
www.theschoolbook.com
t: (+44) 01284 700321

ISBN 1-84549-080-0

Printed and bound in the United Kingdom

Typeset in Tahoma 11/16

This book is sold subject to the conditions that it shall not, by way of trade or otherwise, be lent, re-sold, hired out, or otherwise circulated without the publisher's prior consent in any form of binding or cover other than that which it is published and without a similar condition including this condition being imposed on the subsequent purchaser.

TheSchoolBook.com is an imprint of arima publishing
The ASK Building, Northgate Avenue
Bury St Edmunds, Suffolk IP32 6BB
www.arimapublishing.com

CONTENTS

FOREWORD
Gwyneth Lewis, National Poet of Wales 7

CHAPTER 1
Reception 11

Ein Dydd
Isabella Brewer, Ned Brotherton-Ratcliffe, Mollie Doyne, Jaffa Hay, Charlotte Herdman, James Herdman, Frederick Horvath-Howard, Eva Lantos, Cameron Lewis, Barnaby Like, Jack Swales, Samual Waters 12

My Hand
Reception class 13

Portrait
Cameron Lewis 14
Samual Waters 14
Frederick Horvath-Howard 14
Charlotte Herdman 15
Mollie Doyne 15
Jack Swales 15
James Herdman 16
Barnaby Like 16
Isabella Brewer 16
Eva Lantos 17
Jaffa Hay 17
Ned Brotherton-Ratcliffe 17

Our 'My House' Poem
Reception class 18

When we grow up
Reception class *19*

CHAPTER 2
Years 1 & 2 21

Rwy'n teimlo'n hapus heddiw
Anna Brisland, Theo Brotherton-Ratcliffe, Ben Griffiths, Chloe Cook, Tom Griffiths, Johnathan Gwynne, Edward Fulljames, Penry Herdman, Fred Hayward, Romy Hodges, Abigail Henderson, Hari Hughes, Charlie Henderson, India Hulbert, George Keylock, William Lloyd, Alexander Little, Cerys McNamara, Lisa Moon, Abigail Meredith, Harvey Pawson, Josh Morris, Megan Williams, Lila Phillips, Sean Algar, Bethany Wheatman *22*

Weather
(Frosty, Over the Rainbow, Where's the sun?)
Johnathan Gwynne *23, 35, 42*
Abigail Meredith *23, 30, 33*
Lila Phillips *24, 32, 36*
Sean Algar *24, 33, 34*
William Lloyd *24, 36, 37*
Chloe Cook *25, 27, 39*
Romy Hodges *25, 27, 39*
Lisa Moon *25, 26, 35*
Cerys McNamara *26, 30, 41*
Theo Brotherton-Ratcliffe *27, 32, 36*
Josh Morris *28, 29, 38*
Hari Hughes *28, 34, 41*
Anna Brisland *29, 30, 40*
India Hulbert *29, 38, 41*
Alexander Little *31*
Bethany Wheatman *31, 34, 35*
George Keylock *31*

Megan Williams *33*
Penry Herdman *37, 39*
Charlie Henderson *37*
Ben Griffiths *40*
Harvey Pawson *40*
Fred Hayward *41*
Abigail Henderson *42*
Tom Griffiths *42*
Edward Fulljames *42*

Over the Rainbow
Year One *43*

Frosty
Year One.. *44*

When we grow up
Years 1 and 2 .... *45*

CHAPTER 3
Years 3 & 4 47

Mae athrawon yn dweud...
Bethany Bate, Kearan Morris, Kieran Bate, Lucy Morris,
Finley Branson, Lucy Price, Tom Brisland, Timothy Price,
Freya Felgate, Glenn Pritchard, Billy Ferguson, Hannah Swales,
Jack Griffiths, Andrew Townsend, Alisha Herdman,
Laura Wickham-Charlesworth, Jack Keylock, Ellie Williams *48*

School
(In the Mirror of Memory, English, Yes that would be good)
Hannah Swales *49, 50, 59*
Kieran Bate *49, 53, 58*
Andrew Townsend *50, 61, 62*

Finley Branson 50, 58, 65
Tom Brisland 51, 63, 65
Lucy Morris 51, 54, 63
Bethany Bates 52, 66, 67
Glenn Pritchard 52, 61, 64
Laura Wickham-Charlesworth 53, 60
Jack Keylock 54, 67
Alisha Herdman 55, 60, 64
Timothy Price 55, 64, 68
Lucy Price 55, 68, 69
Freya Felgate 56, 62, 66
Jack Griffiths 57, 58, 63
Ellie Williams 59, 61, 70
Billy Ferguson 66, 67, 70
Kearan Morris 69

When we grow up
Years 3 and 4 71

CHAPTER 4
Years 5 & 6 73

Our Poem/Ein Cerddi
Keiley Adams , Kit Goldman, Jack Bate, Lewis Jones, Rory Branson, James Jones, Wilfred Brotherton-Ratcliffe, Jamie Price, Kelly Davies, Kirsty Price, Joseph Cartwright, Duncan Tindle, Evelyn Fulljames, George Green, Kiah Hodges, Bethan Jones, Emily Lewis, Rebecca Meredith 74

Words and Ideas
(An Evacuee's Christmas Diary, Mind and Body, Good for the Heart)
Keiley Adams 75, 76
Joseph Cartwright 77, 78
Rory Branson 79, 80

Kirsty Price 81, 82
Jamie Price 83, 84
Bethan Jones 85, 86
Lewis Jones 87, 88
Evelyn Fulljames 89, 90
Jack Bate 91, 92
Kelly Davies 93, 94
Wilfred Brotherton-Ratcliffe 95, 96
Kit Goldman 97, 98
Rebecca Meredith 99, 100
Duncan Tindle 101, 102
Emily Lewis 103, 104
George Green 105, 106
Kiah Hodges 107, 108
James Jones 109, 110

When we grow up
Years 5 and 6 111

FOREWORD

I was seven years old when I started scribbling poetry, an epic poem about the rain, and I haven't really stopped writing since. Children before their early teens are natural poets. They have the unfettered imagination, the freshness of vision and lack of fear that gives their work awesome originality and life. Then something happens to most of us, the delight in catching the world exactly as it strikes us gives way to other, perhaps more self-conscious, pleasures.

These poems written by the pupils of Clyro School, with poet Francesca Kay, demonstrate the full and natural talent of pupils who are encouraged to describe the world imaginatively. They show humour, style and vividness of description of which any poet would be proud. When these pupils have grown up, it's quite possible that there will be a future poet laureate of Wales among them. When that happens, I'm only glad that I shall be too old to have to face such stiff competition.

Gwyneth Lewis
National Poet of Wales

Saith mlwydd oed oeddwn i pan ddechreuais gyfansoddi barddoniaeth, epig am y glaw, a dydw i ddim wedi peidio â gwneud ers hynny. Cyn eu harddegau cynnar, mae plant yn feirdd naturiol. Mae eu gwaith yn meddu ar ddychymyg dilyffethair, gweledigaeth ffres a diffyg ofn, sy'n rhoi gwreiddioldeb a bywiogrwydd i'w llinellau. Ond wedyn, mae rhywbeth yn digwydd i'r rhanfwyaf ohonom, ac mae'r dileit mewn dal y byd yn union fel y mae'n ein taro ni, yn mynd yn llai pwysig na phleserau eraill, mwy hunan-ymwybodol.

Mae'r cerddi hyn, gan ddisgyblion Ysgol Clyro, gyda'r bardd Francesca Kay, yn dangos dawn naturiol plant sy'n cael eu hannog i ddisgrifio'r byd yn ddychmygus. Maent yn arddangos hiwmor, steil a bywiogrwydd a fyddai'n destun balchder i unrhyw fardd. Pan fydd y disgyblion hyn wedi tyfu i fyny, mae'n bosibl iawn y bydd yna fardd cenedlaethol yn eu plith. Rwy'n ddiolchgar y bydda i'n rhy hen bryd hynny i wynebu'r fath gystadleuaeth.

Gwyneth Lewis
Bardd Cenedlaethol Cymru

CHAPTER 1

Reception

Our Poem/Ein Cerddi

Ein Dydd

Bore da, bore da.
Prynhawn da, prynhawn da.
Nos da, nos da.
Amser cysgu.

Gan Meithrin Derbyn

Isabella Brewer
Ned Brotherton-Ratcliffe
Mollie Doyne
Jaffa Hay
Charlotte Herdman
James Herdman
Frederick Horvath-Howard
Eva Lantos
Cameron Lewis
Barnaby Like
Jack Swales
Samual Waters

All About Ourselves

My Hand

Here's my hand,
I can
Hold my spoon,
Pull on my shoe,
Wave to my Mum,
I can push the pram for you!

I can cuddle my Mum,
And spin my hand round too,
I can zip up my coat,
How do you do?

I can help my Dad on the farm,
Swim in the pool,
I can help my Mum make breakfast,
How about you?

Oh - and I can help my Mum,
And put my hand into my pudding - yum!

Ensemble poem from Reception class

All About Ourselves

Portrait

My name is Cameron,
I'm a good boy,
My teacher says I'm a whizz kid!

Cameron Lewis

My name is Samual,
I'm a friendly boy,
My teacher says I am caring.

Samual Waters

My name is Fred,
I am a funny boy,
My teacher says I'm always doing something!

Frederick Horvath-Howard

All About Ourselves

Portrait

My name is Charlotte,
I'm a friendly girl,
My teacher says I am a super smiler!

Charlotte Herdman

My name is Mollie,
I am a happy girl,
My teacher says I'm caring and sharing.

Mollie Doyne

My name is Jack,
I am a chatty boy,
My teacher says I'm full of energy!

Jack Swales

All About Ourselves

Portrait

My name is James,
I'm a caring boy,
My teacher says I am her star helper!

James Herdman

My name is Barnaby,
I'm a running around boy,
My teacher says I'm keen to please.

Barnaby Like

My name is Isabella,
I'm a jumping girl,
My teacher says I'm also calm and quiet!

Isabella Brewer

All About Ourselves

Portrait

My name is Eva,
I'm a quiet girl,
My teacher says I am picture perfect!

Eva Lantos

My name is Jaffa,
I'm an excited girl,
My teacher says I'm super at writing!

Jaffa Hay

My name is Ned,
I am a very good boy,
My teacher says I am a little star!

Ned Brotherton-Ratcliffe

All About Ourselves

Our 'My House' Poem

I live in a house with
A white front door,
Cars and a train set,
A big TV,
Lots of toys,
A fish tank with fish,
A tidy Mummy.

I live in a house with
A pet dog Oscar,
My baby brother Thomas,
Spiders everywhere,
A spare bedroom,
A comfy bed.

Who lives in this house?
Well - we do!

Ensemble poem from the Reception class

All About Ourselves

When we grow up

We're going to be
A horse rider,
A teacher,
A Dad,
A policeman,
An artist,
A farmer,
A ballerina,
An acrobat,
A cook,
A ballet dancer,
Another farmer,
And a power ranger!

These are the things
We want to be,
When we grow up,
You wait and see!

Ensemble poem from the Reception class

CHAPTER 2

Years 1 & 2

Our Poem/Ein Cerddi

Rwy'n teimlo'n hapus heddiw

Rwy'n teimlo'n hapus heddiw
Mae'n braf a heulog iawn
Rwy'n teimlo'n fendigedig
Yn y bore a'r prynhawn

Rwy'n teimlo'n drist iawn heddiw
Mae'n wlyb a stormus iawn
Rwy'n teimlo yn ofnadwy
Yn y bore a'r prynhawn

Anna Brisland
Ben Griffiths
Tom Griffiths
Edward Fulljames
Fred Hayward
Abigail Henderson
Charlie Henderson
George Keylock
Alexander Little
Lisa Moon
Harvey Pawson
Megan Williams
Sean Algar

Theo Brotherton-Ratcliffe
Chloe Cook
Johnathan Gwynne
Penry Herdman
Romy Hodges
Hari Hughes
India Hulbert
William Lloyd
Cerys McNamara
Abigail Meredith
Josh Morris
Lila Phillips
Bethany Wheatman

Weather

Frosty

A snowman
Is looking at the snow,
In the hard grass,
I think he wants
to sit on an ice cube.
His name is Mr Happy Snowy Man.

Johnathan Gwynne

A snowman
Is waiting for a friend to come along,
In the frozen garden,
I think he wants
an ice cream.
His name is Snowy Frost.

Abigail Meredith

Weather

Over the Rainbow

I'm going to find
Jumping dolphins in the waving sea,
And a yummy ice cream sundae,
And being with my friends,
Over the Rainbow.

Lila Phillips

I'm going to find
A cute fluffy guinea pig,
Some crunchy crisps,
And my favourite mini motor,
Over the Rainbow.

Sean Algar

I'm going to find
A rhino called Reggie,
A nice big bit of duck,
And my friend Finley,
Over the Rainbow.

William Lloyd

Weather

Where's the sun?

I asked a flower bending down,
I asked a happy slug crossing the road,
I asked a butterfly flying in the sky,
Where's the sun?

I wish I had a big umbrella!

   Chloe Cook

I asked the dripping bull,
I asked the happy worm,
I asked the soaking cow,
Where's the sun?

I wish it would stop!

   Romy Hodges

I asked the soaking wet sheep,
I asked the dripping boy,
I asked the miserable bull,
Where's the sun?

I wish the rain would stop!

   Lisa Moon

Weather

Frosty

A snowman
Is in the frozen garden,
In the snowy grass,
I think he wants a carrot.
His name is Snowy.

Lisa Moon

A snow woman
Is standing
In the freezing cold winter garden,
I think she wants
To move to the Arctic!
Her name is Mrs Frozen.

Cerys McNamara

Weather

Over the Rainbow

I'm going to find
A purring cat,
My Mum's sprouts,
And my favourite toy koala bear,
Over the Rainbow.

Romy Hodges

I'm going to find
A slithering poisonous viper,
Soft yummy ginger cake,
And I'll complete a play station game!
Over the Rainbow.

Theo Brotherton-Ratcliffe

I'm going to find
A cuddly clippety clop horse,
Runny chocolate,
And me going to my baby's christening,
Over the Rainbow.

Chloe Cook

Weather

Where's the sun?

I asked the soaking cows,
I asked the dripping bulls,
I asked a big fat toad,
Where's the sun?

I'm really fed up!

Josh Morris

I asked a penguin playing happily,
I asked a boy and the sun was coming out,
I asked no more because it had stopped raining!

Hari Hughes

Weather

Frosty

A snowman
Is in the snowy garden,
In the freezing ground,
I think he wants
To eat some ice cubes.
His name is Snowy.

Anna Brisland

A snowman is watching,
He is in the garden,
I think he wants to be a real boy.
His name is Frosty.

Josh Morris

A snowman
Is sitting still on the cold ground,
In the freezing garden,
I think he wants someone to play with.
His name is Snowy.

India Hulbert

Weather

Over the Rainbow

I'm going to find
A climbing koala,
Yummy strawberries,
And me, bouncing on my trampoline,
Over the rainbow.

Cerys McNamara

I'm going to find
Beautiful neighing ponies,
And a crunchy apple,
And opening presents at Christmas time,
Over the Rainbow.

Abigail Meredith

I'm going to find
A flying bird,
Runny chocolate,
And a sunny day,
Over the Rainbow.

Anna Brisland

Weather

Where's the sun?

I asked a great big cow,
A hopping frog,
And a huge horse,
Where's the sun?

I am feeling grumpy!

   Alexander Little

I asked a soggy wet dog,
I asked the dripping bull,
I asked the bending flower,
Where's the sun?

I'm bored of this weather!

   Bethany Wheatman

I asked a slimy slug,
I asked a tiny raindrop,
Where's the sun?

I love the sun - where is it?

   George Keylock

Weather

Where's the sun?

I asked the dripping leaf,
I asked the miserable damp horse,
I asked the muddy car,
Where's the sun?

I wish I was at home!

Lila Phillips

I asked the damp old dog with soggy wet fur,
I asked a dripping tree standing tall,
I asked the fast car zooming along the road,
Where's the sun?

I think I'm going to melt!

Theo Brotherton-Ratcliffe

Weather

Where's the sun?

I asked the splashing rain,
I asked the cow who dripped,
The car who squeaked,
Where's the sun?

I wish the rain would stop!

Sean Algar

I asked the yellow daffodils,
I asked a happy dog,
I asked a sad sheep,
Where's the sun?

I like the rain - I don't know!

Megan Williams

I asked a tiny beetle crawling in the grass,
A frog jumping on a stone in the lake,
A bird, the bird was wet too!
Where's the sun?

I wish I was at home.

Abigail Meredith

Weather

Frosty

A snowman
Is looking at fireworks in the garden,
And I think he wants a surprise,
His name is Fab.

   Hari Hughes

A snow woman is looking at the snowy mountains,
In the frosty garden,
I think she wants to sit in the freezer with some ice cubes,
Her name is Mrs Snowflake.

   Bethany Wheatman

A snowman is keeping still,
And looking straight ahead,
And then he saw something!
His name is Andrew.

   Sean Algar

Weather

Over the Rainbow

I'm going to find
A big fat whale,
Hot salty chips,
And me, riding my bike fast!
Over the Rainbow.

Johnathan Gwynne

I'm going to find
Neighing horses,
Runny chocolate,
And my birthday!
Over the Rainbow.

Bethany Wheatman

I'm going to find
A furry dog,
Meatballs yummy,
And my friends who make me happy.
Over the Rainbow.

Lisa Moon

Weather

Frosty

A snowman is waiting for a friend
In the snowy reeds by the frozen pond,
I think he wants company.
His name is Benjamin Snow!

Lila Phillips

A snowman
Is looking at the little boy,
Who is on the solid grass,
I think he wants to be playing with another snowman.
His name is Mr Pringles.

William Lloyd

A snowman is waiting for a friend,
In the winter garden,
I think he wants a new scarf and hat.
His name is Frosty.

Theo Brotherton-Ratcliffe

Weather

Where's the sun?

I asked the wet dog,
I asked a slimy slug,
Where's the sun?

I'm bored of this wet weather!

William Lloyd

I asked a dripping wet bouncy toad,
I asked a soggy bull,
I asked a hoppy rabbit as it went past.
Where's the sun?

I wish that I was Harry Potter!

Penry Herdman

I asked a black crow,
I asked the soaking grass,
Where's the sun?

I wish I had an umbrella!

Charlie Henderson

Weather

Over the Rainbow

I'm going to find
A cute fat guinea pig,
And delicious runny chocolate,
And my birthday!
Over the Rainbow.

India Hulbert

I'm going to find
A cat fishing,
And ice cream,
And me playing with Thunderbirds 1, 2, 3, 4 and 5!
Over the Rainbow.

Hari Hughes

I'm going to find
A giraffe that can reach up tall,
And my scrambler,
Over the Rainbow.

Josh Morris

Weather

Frosty

A snowman
Is looking up to the sky,
In the garden,
I think he wants another snowman to play with.
His name is Frosty.

Romy Hodges

A snowman is standing in the snowy grass,
On the ground,
I think he wants to get a new hat.
His name is Mr Ice Cube.

Chloe Cook

A snowman is looking at you,
In the snowy freezing garden,
I think he wants a ice cream.
His name is Freezing Ice!

Penry Herdman

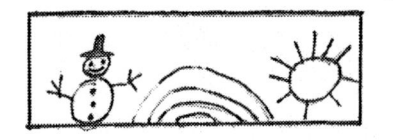

Weather

Where's the sun?

I asked a dripping boy,
I asked a wet soaking sheep,
I asked a dripping wet dog,
Where's the sun?

I wish the rain would stop.

   Anna Brisland

I asked a soaking wet toy,
I asked a wet small sheep,
I asked a miserable slug,
Where's the sun?

I want an umbrella!

   Ben Griffiths

I asked the fluffy clouds,
I asked a snorting pig,
I asked baby blue birds,
Where's the sun?

I like the sun!
It makes me happy.

   Harvey Pawson

Weather

Where's the sun?

I asked a happy, dripping slimy soaking wet slug,
I asked a wet miserable tree,
I asked a damp squelching soaking dog,
Where's the sun?

I wish the sun would come out!

Cerys McNamara

I asked a dripping old dog,
I asked a slimy slug slipping through the grass,
I asked the sheep, I asked
Where's the sun?

I hope the rain stops!

India Hulbert

I asked a squelching slug,
I asked a soaking horse,
I asked a soggy sheep,
Where's the sun?

I wish I had a big umbrella!

Fred Hayward

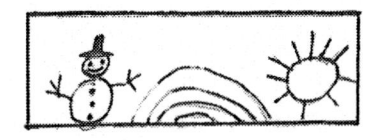

Weather

Where's the sun?

I asked a happy slimy slug,
I asked a wet bird,
Where's the sun?

I wish the rain would stop!

Johnathan Gwynne

I asked dark clouds,
I asked a happy playhouse,
Where's the sun?

I like playing in the rain!

Abigail Henderson

I asked a warty toad,
I asked a shining flower,
Where's the sun?

I'm sad because it's raining.

Tom Griffiths

I asked a happy frog,
I asked a fiery dragon,
Where's the sun?

Edward Fulljames

Weather

Over the Rainbow

I'm going to find
Hot salty chips,
Flying bubbles,
A white fluffy rabbit
And a flying bird that sings,
Over the Rainbow are
My favourite things.

I'm going to find
A fiery dragon,
A stamping elephant,
A snapping crocodile
And an ugly bear,
Over the rainbow
My favourite things are there.

Oh - and more flying birds,
And three fat pigs!

Ensemble poem by Year One

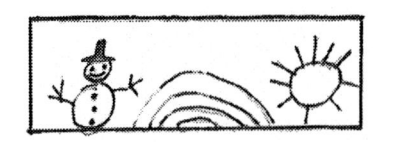

Weather

Frosty

The snowman is
Waiting and watching and looking
On the frozen ground,
He's gazing at the
Clouds and icy pond,
A winter tree,
The frozen snow,
A robin and a little slug,
And he makes no sound.

Ensemble poem by Year One

All About Ourselves

When we grow up

Three artists that paint big pictures,
A helper in a school,
A hairdresser and a doctor,
Our lives will be so full.

A ballerina, karate teacher,
Pony trekker and a soldier,
And a useful builder's merchant,
All this when we're older.

A hairdresser, Harry Potter,
A headteacher, a rider on a horse,
When will we be all these things,
When we're grown up, of course!

A hunter and a soldier,
Train driver, engineer,
In racing cars and vans and trains,
We'll go everywhere.

Working hard in a shop,
A farmer on the land,
A Mum with lots of children,
And giving Dad a helping hand.

These are the things we want to be
When we grow up,
You wait and see!

Ensemble poem by Years 1 and 2

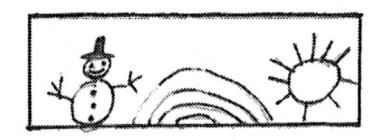

CHAPTER 3

Years 3 & 4

Our Poem/Ein Cerddi

Mae athrawon yn dweud...

Sefwch
Eisteddwch
Dim siarad

Dwylo i fyny
Dwylo i lawr

Cerddwch
Dim rhedeg
Sefwch mewn rhês

Edrychwch
Gwrandewch
Pawb yn dawel

Ffwrdd â ni!!

Bethany Bate *Kearan Morris*
Kieran Bate *Lucy Morris*
Finley Branson *Lucy Price*
Tom Brisland *Timothy Price*
Freya Felgate *Glenn Pritchard*
Billy Ferguson *Hannah Swales*
Jack Griffiths *Andrew Townsend*
Alisha Herdman *Laura Wickham-Charlesworth*
Jack Keylock *Ellie Williams*

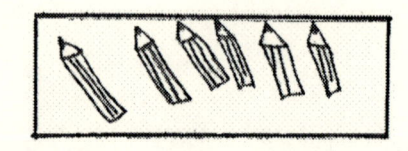

School

In the Mirror of Memory

I see a tiny scared girl,
On my first day at Clyro School,
I remember my Mum dragging me,
I felt a lump in my throat,
Now I wonder what will it be like next year?

Hannah Swales

I see a boy cheating,
On the race track,
I saw that I had cheated,
I felt why did I cheat?
Now I wonder what will happen if I do it again?

Kieran Bate

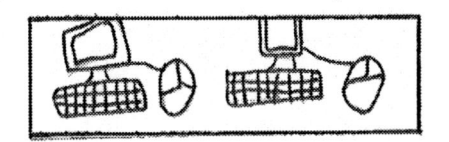

School

Yes that would be good

I think I'd like to
Find out how to hang upside down like a bat,
My teacher saying
"Don't eat any flies, it will spoil your dinner!"

Andrew Townsend

I think I'd like to
Learn how to earn lots of money!
My teacher saying
"Could you lend me a fiver and I'll pay you back on Thursday!"

Finley Branson

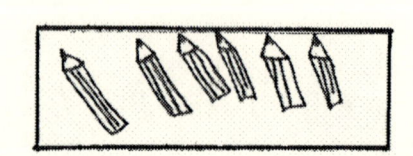

School

English

I can certainly spell extraordinary,
But not so sure about isosoliees!

   Tom Brisland

I can easily spell laughing,
But not so sure about mageniftsint!

   Lucy Morris

I can quickly spell caught,
But not so sure about dicherny!

   Hannah Swales

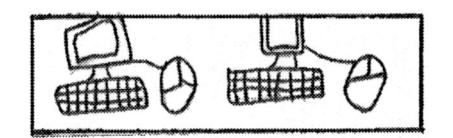

School

In the Mirror of Memory

I see people being told off,
And I was scared it would happen to me,
On my first day I was clinging to my sister at playtime,
I never want to be a new little girl again,
I felt as if scissors were cutting my neck,
Now I wonder if I'm going to be that scared in High School?

Bethany Bates

I see girls and boys splashing in the water tray,
On my first day I made two friends and it felt good,
I wanted to go home, but I did like it,
Now I wonder why I was scared?

Glenn Pritchard

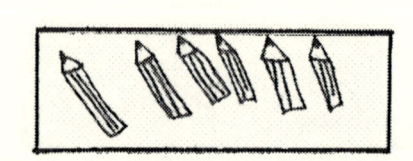

School

Yes that would be good

I think I'd like to
Learn to fly through the air with my hair,
My teacher saying
"Don't go too fast or you'll go bald!"

Laura Wickham-Charlesworth

I think I'd like to
Learn to breathe under the wavy sea,
My teacher saying
"Watch out for those hungry sharks!"

I think I'd like to
Learn to pause the world,
My teacher saying
"Wait, don't freeze me!"

Kieran Bate

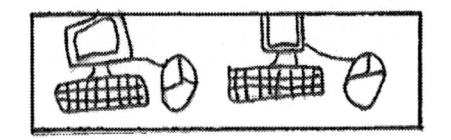

School

In the Mirror of Memory

I see a calm clever Jedi knight,
Dressed up on World Book Day,
I protected all the beings of my school,
I felt very nervous but kept smiling,
Now I wonder what my grown up knight will be like?

Jack Keylock

I see all the children running in the races
On Sports Day,
I was very excited about running in the race,
I felt people running in my tummy,
Now I wonder what was it like there?

Lucy Morris

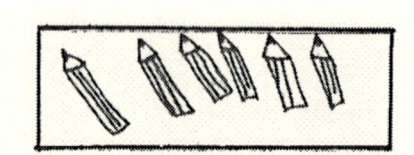

School

English

I can absolutely spell tropical,
But not so sure about expot!

   Alisha Herdman

I can easily spell then,
But not so sure about montin!

   Timothy Price

I can easily spell computer,
But not so sure about redickleos!

   Lucy Price

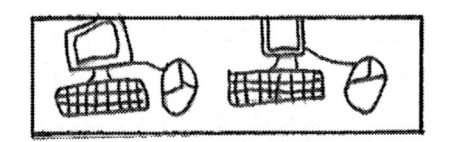

School

Yes that would be good

I think I'd like to
Learn to fly with wings over the swaying ocean,
My teacher saying
"Take a photo of the great white whale."

I think I'd like to find out how to breathe underwater
And try to ride seahorses,
My teacher saying
"Be careful you don't fall off!"

I think I'd like to learn to become invisible when I want,
My teacher saying
"Now you can fly, breathe underwater,
and become invisible,
Go and find a flying lion fish!"

Freya Felgate

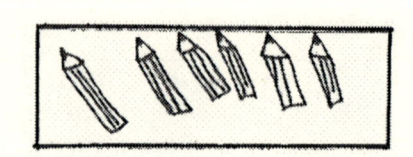

School

In the Mirror of Memory

I see a frightened boy,
On his first day at Clyro School,
I'm glad I'm with Wendy,
I felt scared but excited,
Now I can walk to the football pitch by myself,
Sometimes I climb up the fort,
I have lots of friends to play with,
I like Clyro School.

Jack Griffiths

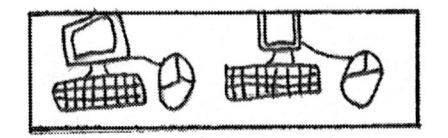

School

English

I can quickly spell calculators,
But not so sure about domnoeise!

Finley Branson

I can definitely spell equilateral,
But not so sure about difalcultee!

Kieran Bate

I can easily spell like,
But not so sure about mycrowskope!

Jack Griffiths

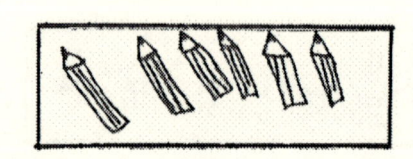

School

Yes that would be good

I think I'd like to
Learn to turn into a twisting turning hurricane,
My teacher saying
"If you don't want to see my knickers, don't blow so hard!"

Ellie Williams

I think I'd like to
Learn to be a millionaire,
My teacher saying
"Don't waste that money to get me a necklace,
Oh no, alright then!"

Hannah Swales

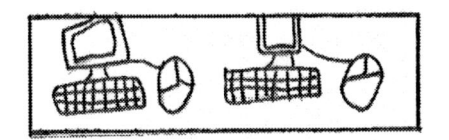

School

In the Mirror of Memory

I see a girl dressed up as a deer,
On the stage at Clyro Court,
I was very excited,
I felt so nervous I was going to explode,
Now I wonder what will happen next?

Laura Wickham-Charlesworth

I see me when I went up to Year Two,
On the day after the summer holiday,
I thought it would be very hard,
I felt scared it was going to be a small class,
Now I wonder what it was like then?

Alisha Herdman

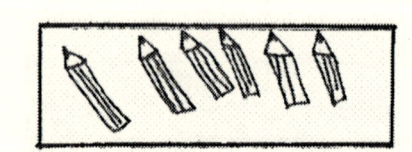

School

English

I can easily spell London,
But not so sure about angerr!

   Glenn Pritchard

I can always spell sheep,
But not so sure about exlent!

   Andrew Townsend

I can easily spell dinonacus,
But not so sure about chrismast!

   Ellie Williams

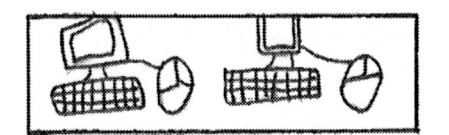

School

In the Mirror of Memory

I see an excited seven year old boy,
On Sports Day,
I ran like the wind and came second,
I felt like an engine driving a car,
Now I wonder if I will be as good next year!

Andrew Townsend

I see me as a flower singing on stage,
At the summer play with the whole school,
I had butterflies and snakes in my stomach,
I felt wonderful once I got started,
Now I wonder if I'll ever be in a play again.

Freya Felgate

School

Yes that would be good

I think I'd like to
Learn to understand animals talking,
My teacher saying
"Stop chatting to the animals and do your work!"

Jack Griffiths

I think I'd like to
Learn to ride a sparkling shining unicorn,
My teacher saying
"Don't get spiked by that horn!"

Lucy Morris

I think I'd like to
Learn to be a piranha,
My teacher saying
"Don't nibble any of your classmates"

Tom Brisland

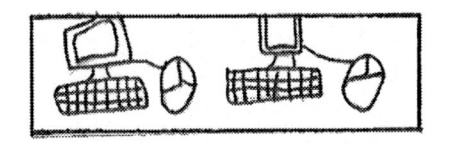

School

Yes that would be good

I think I'd like to
Learn to turn invisible,
My teacher saying
"Where are you?"

   Alisha Herdman

I think I'd like to
Learn to fly like a bird,
My teacher saying
"Watch out you don't crash!"

   Timothy Price

I think I'd like to
Fast forward and rewind time,
My teacher saying
"When should I retire?"

   Glenn Pritchard

School

In the Mirror of Memory

I see a small frightened boy,
On my first day of school,
I hid under the table pretending to be dead,
I felt like someone's fist had punched me in the face,
Now I wonder who that small frightened boy was.

Tom Brisland

I see a small boy with children running round him,
On my first day at school I didn't know everyone,
I was terrified of the Year Sixes,
I felt butterflies in my tummy,
Now I wonder why I was scared of the big children.

Finley Branson

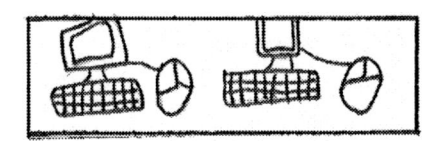

School

English

I can quickly spell diamond,
But not so sure about enthoozason!

Freya Felgate

I can sensationally spell difficulty,
But not so sure about sckammpeey!

Bethany Bate

I can definitely spell but,
But not so sure about lagwigu!

Billy Ferguson

School

Yes that would be good

I think I'd like to
Learn to ride a unicorn round the extraordinary universe,
My teacher saying
"Watch out for the other planets while you woosh by!"

Bethany Bate

I think I'd like to
Watch TV and watch Star Wars Episode 3,
Revenge of the Sith,
My teacher saying
"Jack, do you get this?!"

Jack Keylock

I think I'd like to
Learn to speak twelve languages,
My teacher saying
"What are you saying?"

Billy Ferguson

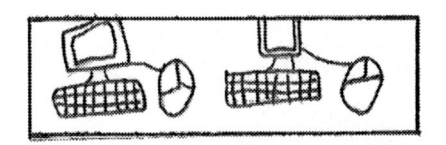

School

In the Mirror of Memory

I see big children and a big school,
On the table I sat on I saw a friend from nursery,
I didn't know many children but I soon met some girls,
I felt like hiding under the table to cry,
Now I wonder why was I so scared?

Lucy Price

I see the big playground,
On my first day of school, frightened,
I made a friend with Andrew,
I felt there was hundreds of people,
Now I wonder where they've all gone.

Timothy Price

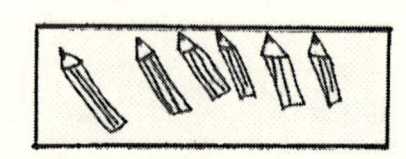

School

Yes that would be good

I think I'd like to
Be a singer,
My teacher saying
"Don't you break the glass!"

Kearan Morris

I think I'd like to
Learn to paint underwater,
My teacher saying
"Mind it doesn't smudge!"

I think I'd like to
Live to 900 years,
My teacher saying,
"Hey, teach me that
but I want to stay young looking"

Lucy Price

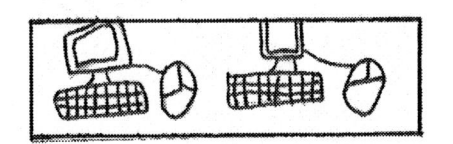

School

In the Mirror of Memory

I see a scared little child,
On the day I started school,
I didn't like it at all,
I felt as if my throat had left my body,
Now I wonder what the next big thing will be?

Billy Ferguson

I see a tiny girl staring at her Mum leaving the room,
On my first day at school,
I thought the room was going to collapse on me,
I felt like my heart had turned to ice,
Now I wonder when will the next time be when I'm as scared as that?

Ellie Williams

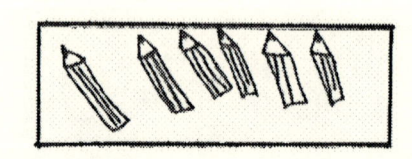

All About Ourselves

When we grow up

A engineer who fixes cars and bikes,
A plumber fixing washing machines,
A horse trainer,
A pop star singing and writing songs,
A quick thinking fireman,
A builder building houses out of wood, bricks and stone like my Dad,
A famous horse rider,
A veterinary nurse working with horses, dogs, and cats,
A farmer feeding sheep,
A story writer, writing stories taking your breath away,
A artist painting pictures,
A crocodile hunter in Australia,
A pilot flying planes as fast as the speed of sound,
A lawyer sending people to jail,
A worker in a launderette washing the clothes,
A actress who works with animals and is not afraid,
A gymnast in the Olympics twisting on the bars,
A teacher with a nice lovely class.

All this in the future,
After school.

Ensemble poem by Years 3 and 4

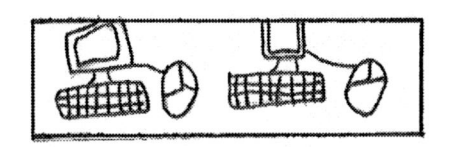

CHAPTER 4

Years 5 & 6

Our Poem/Ein Cerddi

Plant ysgol Cleirwy ydyn ni
Rydyn ni'n hoffi hwyl a sbri!
Rhedeg a neidio, chwarae pêl-droed
Nofio, merlota a rygbi

Plant ysgol Cleirwy ydyn ni
Pydyn ni'n dwlu ar hwyl a sbri!
Darllen, ysgrifennu, arlunio
Ar ôl ysgol chwarae gyda'r ci

Keiley Adams *Kit Goldman*
Jack Bate *Lewis Jones*
Rory Branson *James Jones*
Wilfred Brotherton-Ratcliffe *Jamie Price*
Kelly Davies *Kirsty Price*
Joseph Cartwright *Duncan Tindle*
Evelyn Fulljames
George Green
Kiah Hodges
Bethan Jones
Emily Lewis
Rebecca Meredith

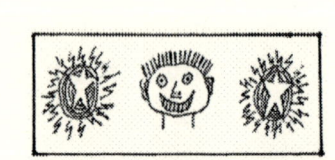

Words and Ideas

An Evacuee's Christmas Diary

It's Christmas Eve,
And it's dark,
It is snowy,
Freezing cold.

I am in my room,
I'm living with Mr & Mrs Wilson,
They sent me up to bed at 8 o'clock,
Today I've been doing more chores,
Cleaning windows,
Making beds and washing clothes.

I remember last Christmas,
When me and my family were all together,
Opening presents.

Keiley Adams

Words and Ideas

Mind and Body

My bedroom is very big,
My sister Megan always messes it up,
So I get really mad!

I love my pet cat,
He is beautiful, cute and very fluffy,
I play with him constantly.

Good for the Heart

Purring cats creep against my legs,
Slithering snakes slide on the floor,
Horses gallop on the hill,
While I run quickly more and more.

Keiley Adams

Words and Ideas

An Evacuee's Christmas Diary

The clock has just chimed eleven at night,
Outside it's windy cold and wet,
I'm sitting in my bed,
I've been picking cabbages all day and my hands are numb,
I'm thinking of my doggy, Harry, I wonder if he's OK?
I wish all the Germans were dead so I could go home.

Joseph Cartwright

Words and Ideas

Mind and Body

If I was a chocolate,
I would have to quickly eat myself,
To stop me from melting!

Good for the Heart

Little rabbits start to hop in the grass,
Birds twittering in the bushes and trees,
Cows mooing in the field,
While I run and bend my knees.

    Joseph Cartwright

Words and Ideas

An Evacuee's Christmas Diary

It's dusk,
The first few stars are appearing,
And they're just like little tiny icicles,
It's raining,
And rain is tip tapping against the window.

I'm in my room,
But is just doesn't feel right,
I feel like I'm frozen,
All I do here is work on the farm,
Eat, drink, and go to bed.

I wish I could be there at my own house,
Eating my turkey,
That's all I've been thinking about
And have been for about six hours,
My Christmas wish is to be at home,
In my bed and for my Mum to say "Goodnight."

Rory Branson

Words and Ideas

Mind and Body

Dragons are swift and beautiful,
Their shiny scales are strong and fierce,
Their fire bright as fireworks.

Good for the Heart

Frogs hop from lily pad to lily pad,
Horses gallop, then over a fence they jump,
Crabs dash over the rocks,
While I run and run with a thump.

The big spiders in Australia creep around,
Dogs run to get a stick,
Monkeys swing through the jungle,
While I go out jogging and my friends take the mick!

Rory Branson

Words and Ideas

An Evacuee's Christmas Diary

It is 8 o'clock in the evening and freezing,
It is Christmas Eve,
It is snowing,
There is a snowman next door.

I am in the living room,
We have a small fire,
But it went out.

I have read a book,
And weeded in the garden.

Some of my friends are still in London,
I hope they're OK,
I wish my friends were with me now.

Kirsty Price

Words and Ideas

Mind and Body

My lovely funny looking pen,
It writes in bold and in small,
But can it write poems?

There are thousands of sweets,
Sherbets, chocolates, are so yummy to me,
So which one to take?

Good for the Heart

Galloping horses dash through fields,
Prowling lions jump for their prey,
Slithering snakes wriggle through trees,
While I run off instead of stay!

Kirsty Price

Words and Ideas

An Evacuee's Christmas Diary

It is late evening and it's pitch black,
It's cold and snowy outside,
I am in bed with the stub of a candle which is slowly flickering out,
I've been feeding animals with hay earlier on.

I remember last Christmas when my whole family
was together sitting around the fire,
I wish I was back with them for Christmas Day.

Jamie Price

Words and Ideas

Mind and Body

Eggs make me serious money,
I'm selling them every single week,
But I don't like eggs!

I don't like pencil sharpeners,
There is always one that never works,
And that one is mine!

Good for the Heart

Fat rabbits hopping through the fields,
Chickens happily strutting in long grass,
Small young lambs skipping carelessly,
While I am in a P.E class.

Slow snails creeping as fast as they can,
Wild wilderbeest in a stampede,
Lions pouncing after prey,
While I cross the finish line a great speed!

Jamie Price

Words and Ideas

An Evacuee's Christmas Diary

The dawn of day,
I'm sitting on my own, writing,
It's freezing,
I'm only allowed to wear the clothes I brought,
I don't really know where I am,
But there's lots of fields,
All I ever do is slave away for Miss Jones,
I remember when my brother used to stroke my hair when I was young,
But I wish my Mum was not dead.

Bethan Jones

Words and Ideas

Mind and Body

The best things are small,
Like stars and numbers and me, Bethan,
Small things are really great!

Good for the Heart

Cheeky monkeys wrecking the car,
The playful dog chases a stick,
Massive jumping cheetahs rush,
While I am not as quick!

Bethan Jones

Words and Ideas

An Evacuee's Christmas Diary

It is midnight,
It's very cold,
and when I breathe out
steam comes out
of my mouth,
The weather it is
very cold,
and a blanket of white
fluffy snow.
I'm in the parlour,
The sharp
North wind blowing,
There's a crack
in the window,
I have been feeding
the dog bringing
coal in and I am polishing the fireplace.
I'm remembering last Christmas
Dad was drinking a glass
full of sherry by the fire,
I wish that Dad survives
in the army and Mum
survives too and I could go home
and the War finishes.

Lewis Jones

Words and Ideas

Mind and Body

My pig is very fat,
She looks like a mad mud zombie,
And eats like a monster!

She weighs a ton,
And she snorts about all day long,
And shines like an otter!

Good for the Heart

Dirty cows plod through the long grass,
Proud horses canter over jumps,
A cunning fox runs through the hedgerows,
While I run and leap over tree stumps.

Lewis Jones

Words and Ideas

An Evacuee's Christmas Diary

It is late afternoon,
It's raining like mad,
Hitting on the roof.

I am lying on a mattress in the attic,
Shivering under a thin blanket,
I have been working on the farm,
Collecting eggs and milking cows.

I am thinking about my life,
My little sister walking for the first time,
My Mum's lovely smile,
I wish the War had never started,
And that I could be with my family.

Evelyn Fulljames

Words and Ideas

Mind and Body

Cats and dogs are tricky,
Which one do I like the most?
Purring, barking, scratching or sniffing?

Good for the Heart

Pouncing cats jump at their toys,
Lions prowl through the plain,
Giggling hyenas run with glee,
While I dance down the lane.

Cheeky monkeys swing through trees,
Kangaroos just love to hop,
Tiny hamsters run on the wheel,
While I swim and swim and cannot stop!

Evelyn Fulljames

Words and Ideas

An Evacuee's Christmas Diary

It's just after midnight,
With horrible icy spine tingling rain,
I am in the cellar,
I have to sleep on the cold hard floor with no blanket,
I've been cleaning out barns full of muck every day,
I only get fed half a bowl of gruel!

I'm thinking about my family,
My Mum, my Dad,
My dead brother who was only 12,
He didn't get evacuated,
And didn't make it to the shelter.

I wish the War would stop,
My brother was alive again,
And that I could go home.

Jack Bate

Words and Ideas

Mind and Body

I really really like trampolines,
You go high, you touch the sky,
It's sounds quite boring though.

Good for the Heart

A rhino charging after a hyena.
A monkey swinging in trees,
A fish dashing through the ocean,
While I'm sprinting away from bees.

A tiger chasing an antelope,
A snail crawling in the park,
A eagle patrolling from the sky,
While I am running through the dark.

Jack Bate

Words and Ideas

An Evacuee's Christmas Diary

It's evening,
It tends to go very cold about now.
It is a freezing snowy wintry night,
I am shivering under my thin single blanket.

I am in the middle of nowhere,
No adults tell me anything,
But I am inside the house,
No other houses around here.

I have been helping decorate the Christmas tree,
It is not a very big one at all.

I should be thinking of home, London, the toasty fire,
Being a family again.

I wish the War would end,
I could go out of this snowland,
Why does Hitler want to kill us?

Kelly Davies

Words and Ideas

Mind and Body
Shoes are very useful things,
Splashing in dirty puddles and messing about,
I leave a track - SMACK!!

Good for the Heart
Little bunnies hop around,
Black horses gallop very fast,
Lions leaping over rocks,
While I hope my ice cream lasts!

Little sheep grazing in the field,
A cat walking through the park,
A hamster running on its wheel,
While I watch my dog bark!

A elephant with its trunk swinging,
A feathery owl out at night,
A jaguar black and so big,
Whilst I fly my colourful kite.

A gorilla growling at a monkey,
A deer sitting down to lie,
A snake slithering quite fast,
While I sit down eating a pie!

Kelly Davies

Words and Ideas

An Evacuee's Christmas Diary

It is early Christmas morning and I've only just got up,
I feel like a snowman I'm so cold,
It's frosty and snow is falling.

The weather is freezing,
I'm sitting on the squeaky staircase in pyjamas,
I've had to do some lambing on the farm,
I've had to push enormous bales of stinking hay.

I'm thinking of my loving mother and my faithful father,
I wish I could just reach out and bring them to me,
I remember playing football with my parents,
They were such a laugh and
I wish I could stay with my Mum and Dad forever.

Wilfred Brotherton-Ratcliffe

Words and Ideas

Mind and Body

I just love my bike,
I love to bust brand new tricks,
But maybe not a backflip!

I quite like my class,
Some people I like more than others,
But everyone's OK really.

I absolutely love custard creams,
I like the sweet sugary stuff inside,
The best bit's the middle.

Good for the Heart

Scaly snakes slithering through the grass,
Cheeky monkeys swing from tree to tree,
Golden lions prowl for pride,
While I ride my bike, that's good for me!

Wilfred Brotherton-Ratcliffe

Words and Ideas

An Evacuee's Christmas Diary

It is early dawn,
It's freezing,
I'm cold,
Outside it's snowy, there's icicles on the window.

I'm in the parlour,
Feeling the cold nibbling at my toes,
I've been chopping wood for the fire,
Remembering my brothers and our fights,
Wishing I was in my own bed!

Kit Goldman

Words and Ideas

Mind and Body

I'm trying to write poems,
But it is not going very well,
So I'm giving it up!!

Good for the Heart

Giant black dogs chase at speed,
Huge bull elephants charging very fast,
Brave golden lions roaring as they chase,
While I run around on the grass.

Kit Goldman

Words and Ideas

An Evacuee's Christmas Diary

It is very late and night and really dark,
It's cold and frosty,
Snowflakes are falling rapidly,
I'm in bed freezing,
I've been feeding chickens
and picking vegetables out of the ground all day,
I'm thinking of me and my family round the fire singing carols,
I wish I could soon be home again and worry free.

Rebecca Meredith

Words and Ideas

Mind and Body

My felt pens are fab,
They are bright and do wicked drawings,
I'm a brilliant artist.

I have a lovely necklace,
It looks like it hasn't been worn,
It's sparkles in the light.

Good for the Heart

Bouncing kangeroos jump around,
Sweet lambs skip to and fro,
Spotty pandas prowl along,
While I am jogging very slow.

   Rebecca Meredith

Words and Ideas

An Evacuee's Christmas Diary

It's shepherds delight,
Loads of stars are about to come out,
It's snowy, white, cold and icy,
I'm sitting on the stair,
I'm freezing,
I've been gathering wood for the fire earlier today,
I've been thinking of my parents all day,
Their smiles when they opened my presents,
My wish is they will be safe.

Duncan Tindle

Words and Ideas

Mind and Body

I have a light saber,
Glowing, gleaming and glimmering in the dark,
I feel like a Jedi!

I have a dog called
Oscar, I'm not sure I like him,
He's just so lazy.

Good for the Heart

Little fish wiggle in the sea,
Big bulls charging at speed,
Huge tusked elephants lying in the sun,
While I am fast enough to run in a stampede!

Duncan Tindle

Words and Ideas

An Evacuee's Christmas Diary

It is midday and very cold,
There are beautiful glistening snowflakes
falling on the windowsill.

Downstairs in my chair
Watching everyone eat a scrumptious Christmas dinner,

I am eating porridge,
Being ordered to get dressed for the guests coming,
Getting very upset.

I'm thinking of my baby brother,
Eating his tasty Christmas meal with Mum,
Away somewhere in the country,
Don't know where.

I wish I could have a present off Dad,
Who's in the War.

Emily Lewis

Words and Ideas

Mind and Body

I watch TV everyday,
It's boring when it's turned off,
So I turn it on again!

Good for the Heart

Fluffy kittens play with wool,
Pretty parrots about to take flight,
Sheep dogs dashing in the woods,
While I go dancing under the disco light.

Slippery snails creeping up the garden wall,
Bouncy bunnies hopping around,
Stampedes of elephants plodding restlessly,
While I go running in the playground.

Emily Lewis

Words and Ideas

An Evacuee's Christmas Diary

It is a dark night with stars like diamonds,
It is snowy outside,
I am 85 miles from London,
I have been running around today,
I am thinking of my Mum lonely in the house,
I wish the War was over and I could be at home with Mum.

George Green

Words and Ideas

Mind and Body

I have a new book,
I will not let anyone read it,
I read it alone at night.

Good for the Heart

Feathery birds flying around and around,
Big brown dogs running at speed,
Black cats climbing over a wall,
While I am running in a stampede!

George Green

Words and Ideas

An Evacuee's Christmas Diary

It is 7.30 and it's Christmas Day,
I am sitting on the tenth step of the staircase,
The wind is going through my hair because the window is open.

It is cold and it is snowing,
The cold hurts my hand is I don't wear gloves,
That is how cold it is.

The people said this is called the country,
The cottage I am in is called Rose Cottage.

I have been playing in the snow with my friends.

I am thinking of last year,
Our Christmas all together,
It was really fun and happy.

I wish the War was over,
And I could see you all again.

Kiah Hodges

Words and Ideas

Mind and Body

I love my little dog,
She can jump one metre, that's high!
I think my dog's cool.

Good for the Heart

Tall horses gallop in the field,
Playful monkeys swing so fast,
Snakes slither through the trees,
While I am running through the grass.

Kiah Hodges

Words and Ideas

An Evacuee's Christmas Diary

Midnight, it is snowing,
Even now I am under my sheet but I am still cold,
It is snowy and cold, frost is on the ground,
I am in my bed far away from home,
They've made me work on the farm,
Feeding all the animals,
I'm thinking of my Mum in London,
With the bombs falling,
I wish I could see my Mum again.

James Jones

Words and Ideas

Mind and Body

I enjoy the beautiful autumn,
I like leaves when they go brown,
It is so autumntastic!

I enjoy the beautiful winter,
I like the amazingly cool cold snow,
It is so freezingly chilly!

Good for the Heart

Horses galloping through the fields,
Cats pounce through the streets,
Snakes slither through the desert,
While I am training to be an athlete.

Lions prowl in the jungle,
Rabbits hop through the grass,
Cows plod in the meadow,
While I run very fast.

James Jones

All About Ourselves

When we grow up

I will be a farmer with 600 hundred acres of land,
I am going to travel the world in a camper van earning money as I go,
Wouldn't it be amazing if I worked in the special care baby unit in Nevill Hall because I like babies, they are so cute,
I'm going to be a S.W.A.T team member.

I will be a farmer who lives on a hill,
And be a stockman who owns cows, sheep, horses and pigs,
So I could look at the farm and make lots of profit,
And show winning stock.

I wish I was a carpenter and make beautiful furniture,
I'm going to be a teacher because I like school,
I want to be a person who sells hot dogs in France on the beach,
I'm going to be a runner like Colin Jackson in the Olympic Games,
I'll be happy to be a child minder because I like playing and looking after children,
I want to be a carpenter because I can make things that I like and sell them.

cont...

When I'm older I'd like to be a nursery worker because I like working with children,
I will have a little shop selling food that I make, and in my spare time I will sell drawings,
I'm going to be a vet and have lots of animals myself,
I'm going to be a nurse because I love looking after and helping people,
I wish to work with dogs, hopefully in the Dog's Trust.

I'm going to be a farmer with lots of animals,
When I grow up I want to join the police force in a busy city,
So there's always something to do.

All this in the future,
After school.

Ensemble poem by Years 5 and 6

Printed in the United Kingdom
by Lightning Source UK Ltd.
107483UKS00001B/187-363